Aligning With God's Promises (Pocket Size)

Aligning With God's Promises (Pocket Size)

Bill Vincent

RWG Publishing

CONTENTS

RWG Publishing

PO Box 596

Litchfield, IL 62056

https://rwgpublishing.com/

Published in the United States of America

1

In the past many years, the Church has had many challenges and difficulties that we face as believers. As a people, some of these challenges are bitterness, resentment, jealousy, and they are having a contaminating influence on people's lives. The scripture warns about how bitterness and one person will defile many. It's contagious. If you watch the news, be careful because much of what you hear is through the spirit of bitterness.

You'll discover that the influence of bitterness will make you become offended easily. When you see that stirring up, make sure that you rise to protect your heart from the contamination of somebody else's bitterness. Both bitterness and jealousy hide under the guise of discernment. It hides under the notion that you see into the heart of the motive of another person. And the Scripture is pretty clear that nobody can know the heart, you cannot use your own heart level to measure the heart of another person, and when we start moving into the area of trying to figure out the motives of another person, we're actually into a distasteful area.

Bitterness is an attachment to the past. Jealousy is an attachment to the past. Jealousy actually works hand in hand with an entitlement that assumes I have certain things in life. So, when somebody else gets blessed instead of me, somebody else has the favorite, the open door, the opportunity, whatever it might be, it makes me feel very less and very insecure in who I am because of their breakthrough and blessing. Jealousy is a contaminant as well.

There is another that I think is the most devastating and the most damaging of all three, and it's called disappointment. Disappointment robs people of the courage for the future. Thought about this disappointment is anchored to yesterday, bitterness is anchored to yesterday, you were born for tomorrow, you were designed to make a difference in this present moment that impacts the course of history, and that's who you are. The apostle Paul dealt with a subject uniquely, two different times one time, he told us in Romans 8, where he was describing that nothing can separate us from the love of God and he goes through, you know, angels can't do it, nobody can do it and then he mentions things present and things to come. Notice he didn't mention the past. Things present and things to come, why? Yesterday can't remove you from the love of God, but it can shut down your awareness of the love of God. Bitterness, regret, disappointment are attached to yesterday, and they are trying to use those things to redefine who we are and where we are and what our purposes are.

Disappointment dislocates a person from his/her purpose and destiny. The enemy works hard to keep us focused on what didn't work so that we're of no use for what could work. Disappointment is the owner of depression. It is depression as a baby, not dealing with it in the early stages deeply affects our emotional, mental, and spiritual health. There's a great verse in Proverbs. It's in chapter 12 or 13, read them both and just keep reading when you're done with those two because it's just all so good.

Proverbs 13:12 King James Version (KJV)

*12 **Hope deferred maketh the heart sick:** but when the desire cometh, it is a tree of life.*

Desire realized is a tree of life; hope deferred makes the heart sick. So what does it say? Disappointment actually makes us vulnerable to spiritual disease. It's like our immune system is shut down in disappointment if we don't know how to strengthen ourselves in those moments, we will be affected by circumstances that didn't turn out the way we wanted. The way we pray, the way we believe for. Many have had all kinds of things happening that were not planned and were never supposed to happen. Disappointments, losses, betrayals, criticisms, all the junk, we've all experienced them. And no one ever likes them, and we're not supposed to. But how we navigate in that adverse situation, the sailboat can actually take the position that sails to advance against the upcoming wind and use the correct attitude heart as the Bible mandates that we should pray and meditate believing that we would actually make personal advancements in the most adverse moments.

In fact, I'd like to suggest to you that what you were born for is on the other end of adverse wins. What you were designed for means the adjustment of the heart, trusting God and learning to trust him, when there are things you cannot control, you cannot explain, trust him in those moments because it will help even though it feels like you're going backward, it actually causes us to advance in the most challenging times. And that's where our strength is meant for.

Disappointment is a thief; it's a thief because it robs us of a sense of vision and purpose. In fact, what happens during disappointment is what people hide behind, who secretly in their heart accuse God of not being faithful. Many would never want to think that consciously, but what it does is it protects that in a wrong way, protects that offense towards God because things didn't turn out the way they were supposed to. I don't think it's possible to get where God has designed us to go as individuals, family units, or as a church family. I feel it's not possible to get where God has designed us to go without us learning how to navigate through this issue of disappointment.

God is the God of promise. There are over 7000 promises in the Bible, So think about this. *When Adam and Eve sinned, the first thing that happened after this since God gave a promise.*

Genesis 3:15 King James Version (KJV)
15 And I will put enmity between thee and the woman, and between thy seed and her seed; it shall bruise thy head, and thou shalt bruise his heel.

Genesis 3 verse 15, he gives a promise of a redeemer. He actually had the promise prepared before there was a problem. Because God is the one who has solutions before we make the mess. Everything was thought of ahead of time, and he set the stage so that we could be restored to him, forgiven of our sins, healed, and our sense of identity and purpose restored. So what we got out of this verse in Proverbs that it says, hope deferred makes the heart sick, but desire realized is a tree of life. So there's the opposite which is the other side of the coin, hope deferred can make you sick. Desire realized, dreams actualized, prayer answered, that whole fulfillment in life is like the tree of life.

Tree of Life was mentioned in three books of the Bible. It was mentioned in Genesis, Proverbs, and Revelation, at least to my way of thinking Genesis talks about what was. Proverbs talks about what is while Revelation talks about what's to come. So the point is, is that the tree of life? If you just turn back to the Garden of Eden, Adam and Eve, they've got a tree of knowledge of good and evil; they can't eat of that one but can eat from all the rest. When they sinned and ate the forbidden fruit, an angel goes to guard them against eating of the tree of life.

The thought behind it is that if I now become a sinner and broke the covenant with God, and I now eat of the tree of life, it won't fix my problem but instead makes me eternally a sinner with no hope for redemption. Never was, it locks me into a pre-determined eternal purpose. So just think with me now, if desire realized is a tree of life, what is it saying? It is saying, part of your eternal purpose is revealed, unfulfilled dreams, and fulfilled desires.

God gives us promises not to be enticed. It is impossible for God to lie, it's not a tease. He doesn't put up false hope, and then causes us to crash and burn, he is a loving father, and this father presents us with promises to inspire and instill in us the capacity to dream. Many believers because of disappointment have lost the capacity to dream. Many believers, because of the loss of promises, have lost the capacity to dream.

Promises are the invitation of God into a relational journey; we're together, we labor to see things happen in the earth, that reveals his nature.

We are in this relational journey, wherein co-operation, we see his purposes manifest in there. Now he can do anything and everything we do better. He could position himself at one place on the planet because every person on the entire planet would hear the gospel as he preached if you wanted to, but he's chosen not to do that because his desire is to work through sons and daughters, why? Because the ambition of God the Father is to be revealed as the Father.

Now, God can show up and reveal himself as the creator, he can reveal himself as love, he can reveal himself as the great judge, he can reveal himself as the Righteous One, the Holy One. But it takes a child to reveal the nature of a father because the father can't reveal himself as the father by himself, there has to be evidence somewhere, just as the creator would create to demonstrate his capacity for creativity. So a father's effect on the well-being of a son or a daughter is what gives proof or evidence that God is actually a perfect, wonderful, glorious Heavenly Father. If you take the gospel of John and you take everything you can find about why Jesus came to earth, you'll have a wonderful list. In first John, it says he came to destroy the works of the evil, and we know that he came to die in our place, we know that he came to redeem us, he came to die and be raised from the dead. We know that He came to initiate the awareness, the realization of the kingdom of God at hand within reach. There's a great list of all the reasons why he came, but they are all sub-points of one primary point.

The Gospel of John deals with it well. Jesus came to reveal the Father. Jesus, who came to reveal the father speaks of the son, through his behavior, reveals who he's related to. In other words, he only does what he sees his father do. He only says when he hears his father say, this is Jesus. So what is he doing? He's revealing the nature of the Father. In fact, the scripture says that Jesus is the exact representation of the Father; there's no deviation at all, an exact representation of the father. So Jesus then tells his disciples, in John 20, it says, "As the Father sent me, I send you." How did the father send him? To reveal the father. How then are we sent to reveal the father? What's the point?

He is revealed for who he is, through your answers to prayer. Tree of life experience. The fact that you and I have this invitation to come before the Almighty God negotiates the wrong words. I'm not sure what it is, but I'll use it anyway, to negotiate over the affairs of man he is interested in input. Promises don't make me God, but they bring me into a relationship where, through my time with him, we negotiate over the affairs of man, so that we can see his will and purposes accomplished in the air. He's looking for that agreement. He's looking for that co-laborer. He's looking for the two to be made one.

In the Old Testament, you can't receive an accusation against somebody unless you have two or three witnesses. It's the many becoming one voice, it is marriage, and the two shall become one flesh. It's when you're born again; you become one with Christ. This whole concept is God takes the many and brings them together into one. The members of the body are called individual members that become one in first Corinthians. So here's this theme. 2Corinthians chapter 1, verse 18, 19 "but surely God is faithful, our word to you was not yes and no. For the Son of God, Jesus Christ, who was preached among you by us, by me, Silas, and Timothy were not yes and no, but in Him was Yes." Now what was Yes? The promises, all right.

All the promises of God, verse 20, "In Him are Yes and they in him amen to the glory of God through us." Hey, that's an awkward rendering. Let me read it to you other than NIV verse 20, says, "For no matter how many promises God has made,.." over 7000, " no matter how many promises God has made, they are Yes In Christ" Before you ever believed a promise, he already determined Yes.

But some amazingly good news for you. Before you ever believe the promise, he said, Yeah, sorry. Let me keep breathing. Yes, it's too, too late. It's too late. You had a chance.

No matter how many promises God has made, they are Yes, in Christ, listen to this face, and so through him, the Amen is spoken by us to the glory of God. So here it is. The father decrees a promise, but he waits for what the co-laborer, the one who says, Amen. The one who comes into alignment with his heart, people say well, my prayers aren't getting answered, then change the way you pray. He doesn't? It doesn't talk to me about what's in my heart; he talks to him about what's in his.

Yeah, discover what it means to seek first the kingdom and all these things will be added. Go to his agenda first and see how he blesses yours and see how he changes yours. So the point is, you and I are embedded in a sense to reveal the father through answers to prayer, which are the breakthroughs. It's the fact that you suffer loss, and it matters enough to you that you get alone with God, and you cry out for the breakthrough so that it doesn't happen again. You have that disappointment; you have that? That person who's got a horrible disease and you prayed, and they didn't get healed, they died. What do you do? You don't just brush it off, you get alone with God, why? Because he gave a promise to you and me, by him demonstrating his life, his love, his power, through his own children. You get along with God to get breakthrough. It's not complicated, but it is challenging.

How do you get a breakthrough? Take risk? What do you do if you don't get a breakthrough? Get alone with God? Then what do you do take more risk? You go into the presence, cry to God whether it's hurting people, and you serve, and you just keep that going back and forth until you, and I learned to do what God's called us to do well. You and I may be stuck at the assignment, but it doesn't give us the right to change this. You are living and breathing because he has hope you will believe for the impossible. You're living and breathing because when the impossibilities of life yield to a son or a daughter, the father is revealed, and he is glorified. He is exalted.

People look at certain things that you and I may do, and they go well because God helped us, not that we're that good. You want to display the nature of the kindness, the heart of God in such a way that people around you are impacted by who he is. Promises invite us to dream. And I'd like to suggest that those who have lost the capacity to dream have lost sight of the promises of God. Our capacity to dream is fueled, inspired by our connection to the promises that God has given to us that we've not yet seen fulfilled.

Yep, it is absolutely the truth.

It is amazing to me that God would want to co-labor because he can do everything better. He just feels impacted by the role that you play, so he actually makes himself vulnerable to the desires of people.

Promises don't make me God. I don't dictate to him what he's to do, but he does invite me into a relationship where I have an influence on what happens. Why would he do that? I don't know. He wants the mark of who you are in him to be seen for what it is. There's something about the nature of God revealed when he uses people like you and me to accomplish His purposes, and that's the invitation. The invitation is for us to believe for the impossible and I'll tell you what, it's been a whole bunch of years now for me and it means it has been breakthrough after breakthrough after breakthrough. You're overwhelmed by what God is doing, and then there's loss and loss and loss. I get along with God and need to say, God, you've got to do something in me because this isn't okay. This isn't okay. It's not okay that this child has this disease. It's not okay that this has happened to this family, it's not okay. It's not okay for my family to be broke. It has to matter enough.

So the disciples saw so many things from Jesus, I can just imagine us being one of the disciples. Can you imagine that little bread and the fish thing you did where everybody got to eat, and there are left-overs? Can you show me that one? Or that walking on the water? That was pretty good did like the storm, but I like to walk in the water? Can you teach me that one? And yet there was only one thing the disciples asked Jesus to teach them which is strange to me because they're with him for three and a half years, they saw all kinds of stuff, more miracles that can be listed in a book anywhere and they asked only one thing for him to teach them. They said, would you teach us to pray? They saw something about his life. He was an expression of this father that he met with on the mountain day after day. And it so provoked them to righteous jealousy that they said, can you just teach us because they saw everything else somehow comes from that. This is a year of increased breakthrough promises that is directly tied to an increase in prayer.

There's this invitation by the God of the universe to come and meet with him. It's in the dialogue with God; if you're not getting answers to prayer, don't change what you pray for, change how you pray, do something because the problem isn't on his end of the equation. If it's not working, it's not him. So you get back to the drawing board, and you say, here I am, again, teach me how to pray. Teach me how to dialogue with you in such a way that things change around me and you're honored and glorified. Do something in me and through me, so that when we talk, transformation takes place. God has invited us into a co-laboring with one that we never could earn for ourselves, a co-laboring role to have an influence on the course of history. And this is why you're still breathing air because you're part of that family, part of that team.

So you've got to be driven by a God-sized dream. If you're driven by a dream that you could accomplish on your own, it's not God's dream. In fact, let me take you to a step further. If you're not overwhelmed by what he has assigned for you to do, you've not heard what he has to say because his assignment is so overwhelming that it compels us to trust. I look at the assignment, and I realized this is not something I can do. So I either ignore the word, or I come into a relationship of trust.

So my prayer and my cry are that God, you would give us grace, for prayer in this next season, unlike any previous season of our life and we permit you to wake them up, *that's cheating*, but it's all right. We do invite you, God, to teach us to pray, we want to step more fully into why we are on planet Earth. The assignment that you've given us in different spheres of life. And I asked the father, that Jesus would be exalted through how we do life and that you, in fact, would teach us to pray.

There's always a chance when we would say they surrendered their life to Christ; they never put faith in Jesus for salvation before, and when they do they would actually be forgiven of their sins and change from the inside out. The Bible calls it being born again. It's changing that happened on the inside of a person that we could never perform on ourselves, but it happens miraculously when people simply put their faith in Christ.

The Bible says whoever calls upon the name of the Lord shall be saved.

Bill Vincent is no stranger to understanding the power of God. Not only has he spent over twenty years as a Minister with a strong prophetic anointing, he is now also an Apostle and Author with Revival Waves of Glory Ministries in Litchfield, IL. Along with his wife, Tabitha, he leads a team providing apostolic oversight in all aspects of ministry, including service, personal ministry, and Godly character.

Bill offers a wide range of writings and teachings from deliverance to experiencing the presence of God and developing Apostolic cutting edge Church structure. Drawing on the power of the Holy Spirit through years of experience in Revival, Spiritual Sensitivity, and deliverance ministry, Bill now focuses mainly on pursuing the Presence of God and breaking the power of the devil off of people's lives.

His books 48 and counting has since helped many people to overcome the spirits and curses of Satan. For more information or to keep up with Bill's latest releases, please visit www.revivalwavesofgloryministries.com. To contact Bill, feel free to follow him on twitter @revivalwaves.

Recommended Books

By Bill Vincent
Overcoming Obstacles
Glory: Pursuing God's Presence
Defeating the Demonic Realm
Increasing Your Prophetic Gift
Increase Your Anointing
Keys to Receiving Your Miracle
The Supernatural Realm
Waves of Revival
Increase of Revelation and Restoration
The Resurrection Power of God
Discerning Your Call of God
Apostolic Breakthrough
Glory: Increasing God's Presence
Love is Waiting – Don't Let Love Pass You
By
The Healing Power of God
Glory: Expanding God's Presence
Receiving Personal Prophecy
Signs and Wonders

Signs and Wonders Revelations
Children Stories
The Rapture
The Secret Place of God's Power
Building a Prototype Church
Breakthrough of Spiritual Strongholds
Glory: Revival Presence of God
Overcoming the Power of Lust
Glory: Kingdom Presence of God
Transitioning to the Prototype Church
The Stronghold of Jezebel
Healing After Divorce
A Closer Relationship With God
Cover Up and Save Yourself
Desperate for God's Presence
The War for Spiritual Battles
Spiritual Leadership
Global Warning
Millions of Churches
Destroying the Jezebel Spirit
Awakening of Miracles
Deception and Consequences Revealed
Are You a Follower of Christ
Don't Let the Enemy Steal from You!
A Godly Shaking
The Unsearchable Riches of Christ

Heaven's Court System
Satan's Open Doors
Armed for Battle
The Wrestler
Spiritual Warfare: Complete Collection
Growing In the Prophetic
Faith
The Angry Fighter's Story
Understanding Heaven's Court System
Restoration of the Soul
Spiritual Warfare Made Simple
Aligning With God's Promises

Web Site:
www.revivalwavesofgloryministries.com

9 788779 678467 3